My First
Holiday abroad

Ann Tracey

Heinemann LIBRARY

Little Nippers

www.heinemann.co.uk/library
Visit our website to find out more information about **Heinemann Library** books.

To order:
☎ Phone 44 (0) 1865 888066
▤ Send a fax to 44 (0) 1865 314091
▣ Visit the Heinemann Bookshop at www.heinemann.co.uk/library to browse our catalogue and order online.

First published in Great Britain by Heinemann Library, Halley Court, Jordan Hill, Oxford OX2 8EJ, part of Harcourt Education. Heinemann is a registered trademark of Harcourt Education Ltd.

Editorial: Sarah Eason and Georga Godwin
Design: Jo Hinton-Malivoire and Tokay, Bicester, UK (www.tokay.co.uk)
Picture Research: Rosie Garai and Sally Smith
Production: Séverine Ribierre and Alex Lazarus

Originated by Dot Gradations Ltd
Printed and bound in China by South China Printing Company

ISBN 0 431 18623 5 (hardback)
07 06 05 04 03
10 9 8 7 6 5 4 3 2 1

ISBN 0 431 18628 6 (paperback)
08 07 06 05 04
10 9 8 7 6 5 4 3 2 1

British Library Cataloguing in Publication Data
Holiday Abroad – My First
910.2
A full catalogue record for this book is available from the British Library.

Acknowledgements
The Publishers would like to thank the following for permission to reproduce photographs:
Alamy **p. 13**; BAA Aviation Photo Library **p. 7**; Bubbles/David Robinson **p. 22**; Bubbles/Nick Hanna **p. 12**; Bubbles/Peter Sylent **p. 11**; Corbis **pp. 4**, **19**; Greg Evans **pp. 14**, **16**, **18**, **21**; Greg Evans/Greg Balfour **p. 10**; Imagestate **p. 17**; Mark Wagner/aviation-images.com **pp. 6**, **9**, **23**; Masterfile **p. 15**; Robert Harding/Guy Thouvenin **p. 14**; Trevor Clifford **p. 5**; Trip **pp. 8**, **20**.

Cover photograph is reproduced with permission of Corbis.

The Publishers would like to thank Philip Emmett and Monica Hughes for their assistance in the preparation of this book.

Every effort has been made to contact copyright holders of any material reproduced in this book. Any omissions will be rectified in subsequent printings if notice is given to the Publishers.

Contents

Setting off

What would you put in your suitcase?

Don't forget your passports – and the tickets and guidebooks.

At the airport

Bureau de Change

Bureau de Change

You can change your money here so you can buy things when you are abroad.

Take your luggage to 'check in', then it's time to go.

Off we go

What can you see out of the plane window?

It's good to be on the ground and out in the sunshine.

Your passport is checked when you enter the country.

A picnic on the beach can be fun.

It's different

Are the signs in the same language?

Is the money the same or different?

Having fun

Mmmmm! Tasty!

It's great to try new food.

People say 'hello' in many different ways.

Things to do

There are exciting new things to do –
riding on a camel is such fun!

There are also beautiful places to see.

Meeting new people

You can make lots of new friends.

Coming home

Let's find something special to take back.

We'll soon be home.

Index

The end

Notes for adults

This series supports the child's knowledge and understanding of their world, in particular their personal, social and emotional development. The following Early Learning Goals are relevant to the series:

• respond to significant experiences, showing a range of feelings where appropriate
• develop an awareness of their own needs, views and feelings and be sensitive to the needs and feelings of others
• develop a respect for their own cultures and beliefs and those of other people
• manage their own personal hygiene
• introduce language that enables them to talk about their experiences in greater depth and detail.

Each book explores a range of different experiences, many of which will be familiar to the child. It is important that the child has the opportunity to relate the content of the book to their own experiences. This will be helped by asking the child open-ended questions, using phrases like: How would you feel? What do you think? What would you do? Time can be made to give the child the chance to talk about their worries or anxieties related to the new experiences.

Talking about holidays
The concept of going abroad to another country is quite abstract for the young child. They can be helped to understand it by pointing out that while there may be differences in the foreign country, like the weather and language, many things will be the same. The exciting aspect of a holiday for young children is often that the adults around them have more time to give them individual attention.

Further activities
The child could cut out photographs from holiday brochures of the country to be visited, draw and colour the national flag and find food imported from that country in the supermarket.